Affiliate marketing secrets

Strategies for Success in Affiliate Marketing

BY

Simeon Favour

Table of Contents:

Chapter 3: Building Your Affiliate Marketing Strategy

- Setting Clear Goals
- Creating a Content Plan
- Utilizing Various Marketing Channels
- Tracking and Analytics Tools

Chapter 4: Content Creation for Affiliate Marketing

- Crafting Engaging and Valuable Content
- SEO for Affiliate Marketers
- Blogging, Videos, Podcasts, and Social Media
- Building Credibility and Trust

Chapter 5: Joining Affiliate Programs

- Finding and Evaluating Affiliate Programs
- Understanding Affiliate Commissions and Payouts
- Affiliate Program Best Practices
- Negotiating Special Deals

Chapter 6: Effective Promotion Techniques

- Email Marketing for Affiliates

Introduction

Welcome to the World of Affiliate Marketing

In the vast landscape of digital entrepreneurship, few opportunities rival the dynamic and potentially lucrative realm of affiliate marketing. It's a world where individuals and businesses come together to create mutually beneficial partnerships, and where savvy marketers can turn their online presence and promotional prowess into a substantial income stream. Welcome to the exciting and rewarding world of affiliate marketing.

The concept is elegant in its simplicity: you, the affiliate marketer, promote products or services created by others, and in return, you earn commissions for every sale or lead generated through your marketing efforts. The beauty of this model lies in its accessibility. Whether you're a seasoned marketer with a wealth of experience or a newcomer with a passion for online promotion, affiliate marketing offers opportunities for growth and success.

The Power of Affiliate Marketing

So, why is affiliate marketing such a powerful force in the digital landscape? The answer lies in its versatility, scalability, and potential for financial freedom. Affiliate marketing offers several key advantages:

Low Barrier to Entry: You don't need a vast budget or extensive resources to get started. With determination and the right strategies, virtually anyone can become an affiliate marketer.

Diverse Income Streams: You're not limited to promoting products within a single niche or industry. The affiliate marketing universe encompasses a vast array of products and services, allowing you to diversify your income streams.

Flexible Work Environment: Affiliate marketing is inherently flexible. You have the freedom to work from anywhere with an internet connection, making it an ideal choice for those seeking a work-from-home lifestyle.

Scalability: As your skills and experience grow, so can your affiliate marketing endeavors. Scaling your income is achievable through various strategies and techniques.

Global Reach: The internet knows no geographical boundaries, and neither does affiliate marketing. You have the potential to reach a global audience, expanding your earning potential exponentially.

Low Risk: Unlike many traditional business models, affiliate marketing involves minimal financial risk. You're not responsible for product creation, shipping, or customer support, reducing your exposure to potential losses.

What to Expect from This Book

This book, "Affiliate Marketing Secrets," is your comprehensive guide to understanding, mastering, and thriving in the world of affiliate marketing. Whether you're a complete novice looking to embark on your affiliate marketing journey or a seasoned marketer seeking to refine your strategies and boost your earnings, this book is designed to cater to your needs.

In the pages that follow, we'll delve deep into the intricacies of affiliate marketing. You can expect to find:

Clear explanations of what affiliate marketing is and how it works.
Strategies for getting started as an affiliate marketer, even if you're new to the field.
In-depth guidance on building your affiliate marketing strategy, from setting goals to tracking your progress.
Insider insights on creating compelling content that engages your audience and drives conversions.

Tips for finding and evaluating affiliate programs that align with your niche and goals.

Effective promotion techniques, including email marketing, social media strategies, and paid advertising.

Conversion rate optimization (CRO) techniques to maximize your affiliate marketing earnings.

A comprehensive look at compliance and ethics in affiliate marketing to ensure you're on the right side of the law.

Strategies for scaling your affiliate marketing business and diversifying your income streams.

Real-life success stories and case studies from accomplished affiliate marketers.

This book is your key to unlocking the secrets of affiliate marketing success. Whether you're looking to earn additional income, build a full-time career, or achieve financial freedom, the insights and strategies within these pages will equip you for a rewarding journey in the world of affiliate marketing. So, let's dive in and uncover the secrets that can transform your affiliate marketing endeavors into a thriving and profitable online business.

Chapter 1: Understanding Affiliate Marketing

Affiliate marketing is a dynamic and rapidly growing field in the world of digital entrepreneurship. In this chapter, we will delve deep into the fundamental aspects of affiliate marketing, including what it is, how it works, the ecosystem that supports it, and the numerous benefits it offers to both affiliates and businesses.

What Is Affiliate Marketing?

At its core, affiliate marketing is a performance-based marketing strategy where individuals (affiliates or publishers) partner with businesses (merchants or advertisers) to promote their products or services. Affiliates earn commissions for every sale, lead, or action generated through their marketing efforts.

Here's a simplified breakdown of the affiliate marketing process:

Affiliate Selection: An affiliate, often a blogger, content creator, or social media influencer, selects products or services to promote within their niche or area of expertise.

Promotion: The affiliate uses various marketing channels such as websites, blogs, social media, email marketing, or paid advertising to promote the chosen products or services.

Tracking: Affiliate marketing relies on tracking technology, usually through unique affiliate links or cookies, to monitor the traffic and conversions generated by the affiliate's marketing efforts.

Conversion: When a user clicks on the affiliate's promotional content and completes a desired action, such as making a purchase or signing up for a service, a conversion occurs.

Commissions: The affiliate earns a commission or a predefined payout for each successful conversion. Commissions vary depending on the affiliate program and product/service.

How Does Affiliate Marketing Work?

To understand how affiliate marketing operates, it's essential to grasp the roles and interactions of the key players involved:

Affiliate (Publisher): This is the marketer or content creator who promotes products or services to their audience. They can be individuals or companies.

Merchant (Advertiser): The business or entity that offers products or services and seeks to increase sales and reach through affiliate marketing.

Consumer (User): The end user who engages with the affiliate's promotional content and may make a purchase or take another desired action.

Affiliate Network: In many cases, affiliates and merchants connect through affiliate networks or platforms that facilitate tracking, reporting, and commission payouts.

Tracking Technology: Affiliate marketing relies on cookies, unique tracking IDs, or other technologies to monitor user interactions and attribute conversions to specific affiliates.

The Affiliate Marketing Ecosystem

Affiliate marketing operates within a multifaceted ecosystem, comprising various elements and processes:

Affiliate Programs: These are established by merchants to recruit affiliates. They provide affiliates with promotional materials, tracking tools, and commission structures.

Affiliate Networks: These platforms act as intermediaries between affiliates and merchants, offering a centralized marketplace for finding and managing affiliate programs.

Promotional Content: Affiliates create content, such as blog posts, reviews, videos, or advertisements, to promote products or services to their audience.

Tracking and Analytics: Robust tracking systems monitor user interactions and conversions, providing data for performance analysis.

Commissions and Payments: Affiliates receive commissions based on predefined payout structures. Payments are typically made on a regular schedule, such as monthly.

Benefits of Affiliate Marketing

Affiliate marketing has gained immense popularity for several compelling reasons:

Low Barrier to Entry: Affiliate marketing welcomes newcomers, allowing them to enter the world of online business without the complexities and overhead of product creation.

Flexibility: Affiliates have the flexibility to choose products or services aligned with their interests and expertise, making it a highly personalized business model.

Diverse Income Streams: Affiliates can promote products and services across various niches, diversifying their income sources.

Scalability: Successful affiliates can scale their efforts, expanding their promotional reach and earning potential.

Global Reach: Affiliate marketing transcends geographical boundaries, enabling affiliates to reach a global audience.

Low Risk: Affiliates don't bear the risks associated with product creation, inventory management, or customer support.

Affiliate marketing is a dynamic and adaptable business model that empowers entrepreneurs to leverage their online presence and marketing skills to generate income. As you delve deeper into this book, you'll gain the knowledge and strategies needed to thrive in the world of affiliate marketing and unlock its full potential.

Chapter 2: Getting Started as an Affiliate Marketer

Embarking on your journey as an affiliate marketer requires thoughtful planning and strategic decision-making. In this chapter, we will explore the essential steps to take as you begin your affiliate marketing venture, including selecting a niche, researching affiliate programs, choosing the right products or services to promote, and building your online presence.

Choosing Your Niche

Your niche is the specific area or topic in which you will focus your affiliate marketing efforts. Selecting the right niche is crucial, as it defines your target audience and the products or services you will promote. Here's how to choose your niche effectively:

Passion and Interest: Start by identifying your passions, interests, and areas of expertise. Choosing a niche that aligns with your interests can make the affiliate marketing journey more enjoyable and sustainable.

Market Research: Research the demand and competition within potential niches. Use tools like keyword research and trend analysis to gauge the interest and potential profitability of a niche.

Profitability: While passion is essential, it's also crucial to assess the niche's profitability. Consider the commission rates offered by affiliate programs within the niche and the overall market demand.

Competition: Analyze the competition within your chosen niche. A healthy level of competition can indicate a viable market, but excessive competition may make it challenging to stand out.

Long-Term Viability: Evaluate whether the niche has long-term potential. Some niches may experience seasonal fluctuations, while others remain consistent throughout the year.

Remember that your niche is not set in stone. You can adjust and refine your focus as you gain experience and insights into what works best for you and your audience.

Researching Affiliate Programs

Once you've chosen your niche, the next step is to research and identify suitable affiliate programs. These programs are partnerships between affiliates and merchants that enable you to promote their products or services. Here's how to research affiliate programs effectively:

Use Affiliate Networks: Explore reputable affiliate networks like Amazon Associates, ClickBank, ShareASale, and CJ Affiliate. These platforms aggregate a wide range of affiliate programs in various niches.

Merchant Research: Research individual merchants and companies that offer affiliate programs within your chosen niche. Look for established and trustworthy businesses.

Commission Structure: Examine the commission rates and payment structures offered by affiliate programs. Consider both the initial commission and potential recurring commissions for ongoing sales or subscriptions.

Cookie Duration: Cookie duration refers to the length of time your affiliate link remains active after a user clicks it. Longer cookie durations provide more opportunities for earning commissions.

Affiliate Support: Assess the level of support provided by affiliate programs, including access to promotional materials, tracking tools, and dedicated affiliate managers.

User Reviews: Seek out user reviews and testimonials from other affiliates who have worked with the programs you're considering. Their experiences can offer valuable insights.

Selecting the Right Products or Services

Choosing the right products or services to promote is a critical decision. You want to align your offerings with your niche and audience's interests. Here's how to select the right products or services:

Relevance: Ensure that the products or services you choose are highly relevant to your niche and target audience. Your promotions should feel natural and authentic.

Quality and Reputation: Select products or services from reputable merchants with a track record of delivering quality and customer satisfaction. Your reputation as an affiliate is on the line.

Demand and Trends: Consider the demand for the products or services and whether they align with current market trends.

Competitive Analysis: Analyze the competition and evaluate whether there's room for you to differentiate yourself in the promotion of these products or services.

Building Your Online Presence

Your online presence is the foundation of your affiliate marketing business. It's where you'll create and share content, engage with your audience, and drive traffic to affiliate offers. Here are steps to build your online presence effectively:

Website or Blog: Consider creating a website or blog as your central hub for affiliate marketing activities. It provides a platform for publishing content, capturing leads, and promoting affiliate products.

Content Strategy: Develop a content strategy that includes creating valuable and engaging content related to your niche. This can include blog posts, articles, videos, podcasts, and more.

Social Media: Establish a presence on relevant social media platforms to connect with your audience and share your content. Each platform has its unique audience and engagement style.

Email Marketing: Build an email list to nurture and engage with your audience. Email marketing can be a powerful tool for promoting affiliate products and building trust.

Search Engine Optimization (SEO): Learn the basics of SEO to optimize your content for search engines and attract organic traffic.

Branding: Develop a consistent brand identity, including your website design, logo, and messaging. A strong brand builds trust with your audience.

As you progress through this chapter and start building your affiliate marketing foundation, keep in mind that success in this field often requires patience and persistence. It's a journey of continuous learning and adaptation, but with dedication and the right strategies, you can build a thriving affiliate marketing business.

Chapter 3: Building Your Affiliate Marketing Strategy

Setting Clear Goals
Creating a Content Plan
Utilizing Various Marketing Channels
Tracking and Analytics Tools

ChatGPT
Chapter 3: Building Your Affiliate Marketing Strategy

Building a successful affiliate marketing business requires more than just promoting products. In this chapter, we will explore the critical elements of crafting a robust affiliate marketing strategy. This includes setting clear goals, creating a content plan, utilizing various marketing channels, and leveraging tracking and analytics tools to measure your progress and make informed decisions.

Setting Clear Goals

Setting clear and achievable goals is the foundation of any successful affiliate marketing strategy. Your goals provide direction, motivation, and a benchmark for measuring your progress. Here's how to set effective affiliate marketing goals:

Define Your Objectives: Start by clearly defining what you want to achieve with your affiliate marketing efforts. Are you looking to generate a certain level of income, build your email list, or increase website traffic?

Make Them Specific: Goals should be specific, measurable, attainable, relevant, and time-bound (SMART). For example, "Increase monthly affiliate earnings by 20% within six months."

Consider Short-term and Long-term Goals: Balance your goals between short-term achievements and long-term growth. Short-term goals keep you motivated, while long-term goals ensure sustainability.

Align with Your Niche: Ensure that your goals align with the niche you've chosen and the products or services you're promoting. They should resonate with your target audience.

Track Progress: Implement a tracking system to monitor your progress toward your goals. Regularly review your results and make adjustments as needed.

Creating a Content Plan

Content lies at the heart of successful affiliate marketing. Your content serves as a bridge between your audience's needs and the products or services you're promoting. Here's how to create an effective content plan:

Understand Your Audience: Gain a deep understanding of your target audience's needs, preferences, pain points, and aspirations. Your content should address their concerns and provide value.

Content Calendar: Develop a content calendar outlining what content you will create and when you will publish it. Consistency in publishing is key to building trust and engagement.

Diverse Content Types: Create a variety of content types, including blog posts, reviews, videos, infographics, podcasts, and social media updates. Different formats appeal to different audience segments.

Keyword Research: Conduct keyword research to identify relevant search terms and topics within your niche. Optimize your content to rank well in search engines and attract organic traffic.

Solve Problems: Your content should aim to solve problems or fulfill needs. Provide solutions, answer questions, and offer recommendations.

Include Call to Actions (CTAs): Encourage your audience to take action, such as clicking on affiliate links, subscribing to your email list, or making a purchase. Use clear and compelling CTAs.

Utilizing Various Marketing Channels

Successful affiliate marketers often diversify their marketing channels to reach a broader audience. Here are some marketing channels to consider:

Website/Blog: Your website or blog serves as your primary platform for creating and sharing content.

Social Media: Establish a presence on social media platforms relevant to your niche. Share content, engage with your audience, and promote affiliate products.

Email Marketing: Build and nurture an email list to connect with your audience on a more personal level. Email marketing can be highly effective for affiliate promotions.

Paid Advertising: Consider using paid advertising platforms like Google Ads or Facebook Ads to drive targeted traffic to your affiliate offers. Ensure your ad campaigns align with your goals and budget.

YouTube: Create video content on YouTube, one of the largest search engines, to reach a wide audience.

Podcasting: If your niche suits audio content, consider starting a podcast to share valuable insights and affiliate recommendations.

Tracking and Analytics Tools

Effective affiliate marketing relies on data-driven decision-making. Utilize tracking and analytics tools to measure your performance and gather insights. Here are some essential tools and metrics to consider:

Google Analytics: Monitor website traffic, user behavior, and conversions on your website.

Affiliate Program Analytics: Most affiliate programs provide analytics tools to track clicks, conversions, and commissions.

Conversion Rate: Measure the percentage of visitors who take the desired action, such as making a purchase or signing up.

Click-Through Rate (CTR): Track the percentage of clicks on your affiliate links compared to the number of times they were shown.

Earnings per Click (EPC): Calculate the average earnings generated per click on your affiliate links.

Return on Investment (ROI): Determine the return on investment for paid advertising campaigns.

Email Open and Click Rates: Monitor email engagement metrics to assess the effectiveness of your email marketing efforts.

Social Media Insights: Analyze engagement, reach, and conversion metrics on social media platforms.

By regularly reviewing these metrics and adjusting your strategies accordingly, you can optimize your affiliate marketing efforts for better results.

As you work through this chapter, remember that affiliate marketing is both an art and a science. Crafting a well-defined strategy, consistently creating valuable content, and analyzing data are essential components of success in this dynamic field.

Chapter 4: Content Creation for Affiliate Marketing

Content is the lifeblood of affiliate marketing. In this chapter, we will delve into the art and science of creating compelling content that resonates with your audience, drives traffic, and ultimately leads to conversions. This chapter covers crafting engaging and valuable content, optimizing for search engines (SEO), utilizing various content formats (blogging, videos, podcasts, and social media), and building credibility and trust.

Crafting Engaging and Valuable Content

Successful affiliate marketers understand the importance of creating content that adds value to their audience's lives. Here's how to craft engaging and valuable content:

Know Your Audience: Start by understanding your audience's needs, interests, and pain points.

Your content should address their specific challenges and provide solutions.

Quality Over Quantity: Focus on creating high-quality content rather than churning out large volumes. Quality content builds trust and credibility.

Originality: Offer unique perspectives and insights. Avoid duplicating content that's already widely available.

Value Proposition: Clearly communicate the value of your content to your audience. Explain what readers or viewers will gain from consuming it.

Engagement: Encourage interaction and engagement. Ask questions, invite comments, and respond to your audience's feedback.

Storytelling: Incorporate storytelling into your content. Personal anecdotes and narratives can resonate deeply with your audience.

SEO for Affiliate Marketers

Search engine optimization (SEO) is essential for driving organic traffic to your affiliate content. Here's how to optimize your content effectively:

Keyword Research: Identify relevant keywords and phrases related to your niche and products. Use keyword research tools to find valuable keywords with good search volume and low competition.

On-Page SEO: Optimize your content for on-page SEO by incorporating keywords naturally into your titles, headings, and throughout the content. Ensure your content is well-structured and easy to read.

Quality Backlinks: Earn high-quality backlinks from reputable websites in your niche. Backlinks boost your content's authority and search engine ranking.

Mobile Optimization: Ensure your website and content are mobile-friendly, as mobile optimization is a significant ranking factor.

Site Speed: Improve your website's loading speed. Faster websites tend to rank higher in search results.

Regular Updates: Keep your content updated and fresh. Search engines favor up-to-date content.

Blogging, Videos, Podcasts, and Social Media

Affiliate marketers have a range of content formats to choose from. Here's how to utilize various content types effectively:

Blogging: Maintain a blog as a central hub for your content. Write informative blog posts that provide value to your audience and incorporate affiliate links naturally.

Videos: Create video content on platforms like YouTube. Videos are highly engaging and can effectively showcase products or services.

Podcasts: Start a podcast if your niche aligns with audio content. Podcasts are a great way to build a dedicated audience.

Social Media: Leverage social media platforms to share content, engage with your audience, and promote affiliate products. Each platform has its unique audience and engagement style.

Email Marketing: Send out email newsletters featuring affiliate recommendations. Email marketing can be highly effective for conversions.

Building Credibility and Trust

Building credibility and trust with your audience is paramount in affiliate marketing. Here's how to establish yourself as a trusted affiliate marketer:

Honesty and Transparency: Be honest about your affiliate relationships. Clearly disclose when you're promoting affiliate products.

Expertise: Demonstrate your expertise in your niche. Provide valuable insights and recommendations based on your knowledge.

Product Knowledge: Thoroughly research and understand the products or services you're promoting. Only recommend those you genuinely believe in.

User Reviews and Testimonials: Share user reviews and testimonials for products or services you've personally used. Authentic feedback builds trust.

Consistency: Consistently deliver valuable content and engage with your audience. Reliability fosters trust.

Personal Branding: Build a personal brand that reflects your values and expertise. A strong brand can enhance credibility.

As you navigate this chapter, remember that content creation is an ongoing process. Regularly assess the performance of your content and make refinements based on audience feedback and analytics data. Building credibility and trust takes time, but it's a crucial foundation for long-term success in affiliate marketing.

Chapter 5: Joining Affiliate Programs

Joining the right affiliate programs is a pivotal step in your affiliate marketing journey. In this chapter, we will explore the process of finding and evaluating affiliate programs, understanding affiliate commissions and payouts, best practices for affiliate program participation, and tips for negotiating special deals with merchants.

Finding and Evaluating Affiliate Programs

When it comes to affiliate programs, quality and alignment with your niche are key. Here's how to find and evaluate affiliate programs effectively:

Affiliate Networks: Start by exploring reputable affiliate networks such as Amazon Associates, ClickBank, ShareASale, and CJ Affiliate. These platforms host a wide range of affiliate programs in various niches.

Merchant Research: Research individual merchants and companies in your niche to see if they offer affiliate programs. Look for established and trustworthy businesses.

Product Relevance: Ensure that the products or services offered through the affiliate program align with your niche and audience's interests. Relevance is essential for conversions.

Commission Structure: Examine the commission rates and payment structures offered by affiliate programs. Consider both initial commissions and potential recurring commissions for ongoing sales or subscriptions.

Cookie Duration: Check the duration of the affiliate program's tracking cookies. Longer cookie durations provide more opportunities for earning commissions from repeat visitors.

Affiliate Support: Assess the level of support provided by affiliate programs, including access to promotional materials, tracking tools, and dedicated affiliate managers.

User Reviews: Seek out user reviews and testimonials from other affiliates who have worked with the programs you're considering. Their experiences can offer valuable insights.

Understanding Affiliate Commissions and Payouts

Commissions and payouts are at the core of affiliate marketing. Here's how to understand them effectively:

Commission Types: Affiliate programs offer various commission types, including:

Pay-Per-Sale (PPS): You earn a commission when a referred user makes a purchase.
Pay-Per-Lead (PPL): You earn a commission when a referred user takes a specific action, such as signing up for a newsletter.
Pay-Per-Click (PPC): You earn a commission based on the number of clicks generated through your affiliate links.

Commission Rates: Different products and services offer different commission rates. Some may offer fixed amounts, while others provide a percentage of the sale. Evaluate the potential earnings based on these rates.

Payment Threshold: Affiliate programs often have a payment threshold. You must reach a certain earnings level before receiving a payout.

Payment Methods: Understand the payment methods available (e.g., bank transfer, PayPal, check) and choose the one that suits your preferences.

Payment Schedule: Familiarize yourself with the program's payment schedule. Some programs pay monthly, while others have different payout frequencies.

Affiliate Program Best Practices

Participating in affiliate programs requires a strategic approach. Here are some best practices to keep in mind:

Diversify Programs: Join multiple affiliate programs to diversify your income sources and reduce reliance on a single program.

Disclose Affiliation: Always disclose your affiliate relationship transparently to your audience. Honesty builds trust.

Promote What You Believe In: Focus on promoting products or services you genuinely believe in and would recommend to friends or family.

Track Performance: Use tracking and analytics tools to monitor the performance of each affiliate program. Evaluate which programs are delivering the best results.

Stay Updated: Keep up with program changes, promotions, and seasonal opportunities to maximize your earnings.

Negotiating Special Deals

In some cases, you may have the opportunity to negotiate special deals with merchants. Here are tips for successful negotiations:

Establish Trust: Build a strong relationship with the merchant by consistently delivering quality traffic and conversions.

Highlight Your Value: Showcase the value you bring to the merchant, such as your audience size, engagement, and conversion rates.

Propose Win-Win Deals: Present proposals that benefit both you and the merchant. This could include exclusive discounts or promotions for your audience.

Be Professional: Approach negotiations professionally and with a clear understanding of your worth as an affiliate.

Document Agreements: Once an agreement is reached, document the terms and conditions in writing to avoid misunderstandings.

Joining affiliate programs is a crucial aspect of your affiliate marketing strategy. By carefully evaluating programs, understanding commission structures, following best practices, and occasionally negotiating special deals, you can optimize your affiliate partnerships and increase your chances of success in the affiliate marketing landscape.

Chapter 6: Effective Promotion Techniques

Promoting affiliate products effectively requires a strategic approach and a variety of techniques. In this chapter, we will explore some of the most powerful promotion methods available to affiliate marketers. These include email marketing, social media promotion strategies, paid advertising, and building an affiliate marketing sales funnel.

Email Marketing for Affiliates

Email marketing is a highly effective tool for affiliate marketers to engage with their audience and promote products or services. Here's how to harness the power of email marketing:

Build and Segment Your Email List: Start by building a quality email list of subscribers interested in your niche. Segment your list based on interests and behaviors to send targeted promotions.

Provide Value: Before promoting affiliate products, provide valuable content to your subscribers. This builds trust and positions you as an authority in your niche.

Strategic Promotions: When promoting affiliate products via email, ensure your promotions are well-timed and relevant to your subscribers. Use compelling subject lines and clear calls to action (CTAs).

A/B Testing: Experiment with different email formats, CTAs, and content to see what resonates best with your audience. A/B testing can help you optimize your email campaigns.

Automation: Implement email automation to send personalized messages based on user actions. This can include welcome sequences, abandoned cart reminders, and follow-up emails.

Compliance: Ensure your email marketing practices comply with relevant regulations, such as the CAN-SPAM Act or GDPR, depending on your audience's location.

Social Media Promotion Strategies

Social media platforms offer vast opportunities for affiliate promotion. Here are strategies for effective social media promotion:

Choose the Right Platforms: Select social media platforms that align with your niche and audience. Each platform has its unique demographics and engagement style.

Engagement and Interaction: Actively engage with your followers by responding to comments, questions, and messages. Build a community around your niche.

Content Variety: Share diverse content types, including product reviews, how-to guides, videos, and engaging stories. Adapt your content to suit each platform.

Promotional Posts: Integrate affiliate promotions naturally into your social media content. Use eye-catching visuals and compelling captions.

Leverage Hashtags: Use relevant hashtags to expand the reach of your posts and increase discoverability.

Collaborations: Partner with other influencers or affiliates in your niche for joint promotions or shout-outs.

Analytics: Analyze social media analytics to understand which content and promotions resonate best with your audience. Adjust your strategy accordingly.

Paid Advertising for Affiliates

Paid advertising can accelerate your affiliate marketing efforts by driving targeted traffic to your promotions. Here's how to use paid advertising effectively:

Select the Right Platform: Choose advertising platforms that align with your niche and target audience. Options include Google Ads, Facebook Ads, Instagram Ads, and more.

Keyword Research: Conduct keyword research to identify relevant keywords and phrases to target in your ads. This is crucial for search engine advertising.

Ad Creatives: Create compelling ad creatives that include attention-grabbing headlines, clear product descriptions, and persuasive CTAs.

Budget Management: Set a realistic budget for your advertising campaigns and monitor spending carefully. Optimize campaigns based on performance data.

Conversion Tracking: Implement conversion tracking to measure the effectiveness of your ads in driving affiliate conversions.

Testing and Optimization: Continuously A/B test different ad variations, targeting options, and ad copy to improve campaign performance.

Building an Affiliate Marketing Sales Funnel

A well-structured sales funnel can guide your audience from initial awareness to conversion. Here's how to build an affiliate marketing sales funnel:

Awareness: Attract your target audience's attention through blog posts, social media content, or lead magnets that provide value and introduce them to the problem or need.

Interest: Engage your audience's interest by delivering more in-depth content, such as guides, videos, or webinars, that addresses their specific challenges.

Desire: Create a desire for the affiliate product by showcasing its benefits, features, and how it solves the audience's problem.

Action: Encourage action by providing clear affiliate links, promotions, and compelling CTAs that guide the audience toward making a purchase or taking the desired action.

Follow-Up: Implement email follow-up sequences that nurture leads and encourage them to complete the desired action.

Measurement: Analyze the performance of your sales funnel at each stage and make necessary adjustments to improve conversion rates.

Effective promotion techniques are at the core of successful affiliate marketing. By mastering email marketing, leveraging social media platforms, using paid advertising strategically, and building an efficient sales funnel, you can maximize your affiliate earnings and provide value to your audience simultaneously.

Chapter 7: Maximizing Conversions

Conversions are the ultimate goal in affiliate marketing. In this chapter, we will explore techniques and strategies for maximizing conversions, including Conversion Rate Optimization (CRO), crafting compelling Calls to Action (CTAs), boosting click-through rates, and conducting split testing and optimization.

Conversion Rate Optimization (CRO)

Conversion Rate Optimization (CRO) is the process of enhancing your affiliate marketing strategies to increase the percentage of visitors who take the desired action, such as making a purchase or signing up. Here's how to implement CRO effectively:

Analyzing User Behavior: Use analytics tools to understand how users navigate your website and interact with your affiliate content. Identify potential barriers to conversion.

A/B Testing: Conduct A/B tests to compare different versions of your content or CTAs. Test elements like headlines, images, and button colors to see which performs better.

Optimize Landing Pages: Ensure that your landing pages are designed for conversion. Simplify the layout, use clear and persuasive copy, and minimize distractions.

Mobile Optimization: With the increasing use of mobile devices, it's essential to optimize your affiliate content and landing pages for mobile users.

Page Load Speed: Improve the loading speed of your website. Slow-loading pages can deter users from taking action.

Clear Value Proposition: Clearly communicate the value of the affiliate product or service. Explain how it addresses the user's problem or need.

Crafting Compelling Calls to Action (CTAs)

Calls to Action (CTAs) are crucial for guiding users toward conversion. Crafting compelling CTAs is an art in itself. Here are some tips:

Be Action-Oriented: Use action verbs in your CTAs to prompt users to take immediate action, such as "Buy Now," "Get Started," or "Sign Up Today."

Highlight Benefits: Mention the benefits users will gain from taking the desired action. For example, "Join our newsletter for exclusive tips."

Create a Sense of Urgency: Encourage immediate action by adding a sense of urgency, such as "Limited-time offer" or "Last chance."

Make CTAs Stand Out: Use contrasting colors and design elements to make your CTAs visually prominent.

Placement Matters: Position your CTAs strategically, both within your content and on your landing pages. Make sure they are easily accessible.

Personalization: Consider personalizing CTAs based on user behavior or demographics to increase relevance.

Strategies for Boosting Click-Through Rates

Click-through rates (CTR) are an essential metric in affiliate marketing, indicating the effectiveness of your affiliate links and promotions. Here are strategies for boosting CTR:

Relevance: Ensure that your affiliate promotions are highly relevant to the content surrounding them. Users are more likely to click on links that align with their interests.

Use Eye-Catching Visuals: Incorporate attention-grabbing images and graphics alongside your affiliate links to draw users' attention.

Position Promotions Strategically: Place affiliate promotions where they naturally fit within your content. For example, product recommendations within relevant blog posts.

Leverage Social Proof: Highlight positive reviews, testimonials, or user ratings to build trust and encourage clicks.

Experiment with Link Formats: Test different link formats, such as text links, image links, and buttons, to see which resonates best with your audience.

Create Curiosity: Craft headlines and descriptions that pique users' curiosity or address a specific problem they may have.

Split Testing and Optimization

Split testing, also known as A/B testing, is a valuable technique for optimizing your affiliate marketing efforts. Here's how to approach split testing:

Identify Variables: Choose specific elements to test, such as headlines, images, CTAs, or even entire landing pages.

Create Variations: Develop multiple versions (A and B) with one differing element. Keep everything else the same for a fair comparison.

Run the Test: Implement the variations and run the test with a portion of your audience to see which version performs better.

Analyze Results: Evaluate the data to determine which version generated higher conversions or CTR.

Implement Changes: Apply the winning variation to your affiliate content and continue testing other elements for continuous improvement.

By implementing these strategies and regularly optimizing your affiliate content and promotions, you can increase your conversion rates, drive more affiliate earnings, and provide a better experience for your audience.

Chapter 8: Compliance and Ethics in Affiliate Marketing

Operating within legal and ethical boundaries is paramount in affiliate marketing. In this chapter, we will explore the essential aspects of compliance and ethics in affiliate marketing, including legal and ethical considerations, the importance of disclosures and transparency, common pitfalls to avoid, and staying on the right side of regulations.

Legal and Ethical Considerations

Affiliate marketers must be aware of the legal and ethical considerations that govern their industry. Here are some key considerations:

Truthful Advertising: Advertisements, content, and promotions must be truthful and not contain false or misleading information about the affiliate product or service.

Consumer Protection: Comply with consumer protection laws and regulations, ensuring that consumers are not deceived or harmed by your promotions.

Copyright and Trademarks: Respect intellectual property rights, including copyrights and trademarks, when using images, text, or branding in your content.

Privacy: Protect user privacy by adhering to data protection laws and obtaining consent when collecting personal information.

Endorsements and Testimonials: Clearly disclose any material connections, endorsements, or compensation received in exchange for promoting products. Transparency is key.

Disclosures and Transparency

Transparency is essential to maintaining trust with your audience. Here's how to approach disclosures and transparency:

Clear Disclosures: Disclose your affiliate relationship conspicuously in your content, such as blog posts, reviews, social media posts, and videos. Use clear and unambiguous language.

Affiliate Links: Clearly label affiliate links as such, using phrases like "Affiliate Link" or "Disclosure."

Honest Reviews: If you provide product reviews or testimonials, ensure they are honest and based on your genuine experiences. Disclose if you receive compensation for reviews.

Privacy Policy: Have a privacy policy on your website that explains how user data is collected, used, and protected.

Compliance with Regulations: Familiarize yourself with affiliate marketing regulations in your region and adhere to them. Regulations may vary by country or state.

Avoiding Common Pitfalls

Affiliate marketers often encounter common pitfalls that can negatively impact their reputation and legal standing. Here are some pitfalls to avoid:

Deceptive Practices: Avoid deceptive tactics, such as fake reviews, false claims, or click fraud, which can lead to legal consequences.

Keyword Stuffing: Refrain from keyword stuffing in your content, as it can lead to poor user experience and search engine penalties.

Unsolicited Email Marketing: Abide by anti-spam laws and obtain consent before sending promotional emails to users.

Inadequate Disclosures: Failing to disclose your affiliate relationship or compensation can erode trust with your audience and lead to legal issues.

Failure to Update Content: Keep your content up-to-date and remove outdated promotions or affiliate links to avoid misleading your audience.

Staying on the Right Side of Regulations

To ensure compliance with regulations in affiliate marketing, consider the following steps:

Research Regulations: Thoroughly research the affiliate marketing regulations in your region and any regions where your audience resides.

Consult Legal Advice: If in doubt, seek legal counsel or advice from professionals experienced in affiliate marketing and relevant regulations.

Regularly Review and Update: Stay informed about changes in regulations and adjust your practices accordingly. Compliance is an ongoing process.

Network with Affiliates: Join affiliate marketing communities or forums to share insights and stay updated on industry best practices.

By prioritizing compliance and ethics in your affiliate marketing endeavors, you not only protect yourself from legal issues but also build a reputation as a trustworthy and credible affiliate marketer. Transparency and adherence to regulations are integral to long-term success in this field.

Chapter 9: Scaling Your Affiliate Marketing Business

Scaling your affiliate marketing business is the key to achieving sustainable growth and increased earnings. In this chapter, we will explore strategies for scaling your affiliate marketing business effectively, including expanding your reach, hiring and outsourcing, diversifying your income streams, and staying updated and adaptable.

Expanding Your Reach

Expanding your reach is essential for reaching a larger audience and increasing your affiliate earnings. Here's how to do it:

Content Expansion: Continue to produce high-quality, relevant content that resonates with your audience. Regularly publish new content to attract new visitors and retain existing ones.

Keyword Research: Conduct keyword research to identify new topics and niches within your industry that have the potential for high search volume and low competition.

Guest Posting: Collaborate with other websites or bloggers in your niche to publish guest posts. This exposes your content to a wider audience and can lead to valuable backlinks.

Social Media Marketing: Increase your presence on social media platforms, engage with your audience, and share your affiliate content to drive more traffic.

Email Marketing: Grow your email list and implement effective email marketing strategies to reach your subscribers with relevant promotions.

Paid Advertising: Consider investing in paid advertising campaigns, such as Google Ads or Facebook Ads, to target specific keywords or demographics and expand your audience.

Hiring and Outsourcing

As your affiliate marketing business grows, you may need to delegate certain tasks to maintain efficiency. Here's how to approach hiring and outsourcing:

Identify Tasks: Determine which tasks can be outsourced or delegated, such as content creation, SEO, or administrative work.

Hiring Freelancers: Consider hiring freelancers or contractors with expertise in specific areas to help with content production, graphic design, or technical aspects of your website.

Virtual Assistants: Virtual assistants can handle administrative tasks, email management, and other routine activities, freeing up your time for strategic efforts.

Affiliate Managers: If you work with multiple affiliate programs, hiring an affiliate manager can help you manage partnerships, track performance, and negotiate deals.

Diversifying Your Income Streams

Relying solely on one affiliate program or revenue source can be risky. Diversify your income streams to ensure financial stability:

Multiple Affiliate Programs: Partner with multiple affiliate programs in different niches to spread your earnings across various products or services.

Product Creation: Consider creating and selling your own digital products, such as e-books or online courses, to generate additional income.

Membership Sites: Develop membership sites or paid communities where you offer exclusive content or services for a recurring fee.

Consulting or Coaching: If you possess expertise in your niche, offer consulting or coaching services to individuals or businesses.

Ad Revenue: Incorporate display ads or sponsored content on your website to generate ad revenue in addition to affiliate earnings.

Staying Updated and Adapting

The affiliate marketing landscape is dynamic, and staying updated is crucial for continued success:

Continuous Learning: Invest in your education by staying informed about industry trends, new marketing techniques, and changes in regulations.

Networking: Attend affiliate marketing conferences, webinars, and forums to network with industry professionals and gain insights into emerging opportunities.

Adaptability: Be adaptable and open to trying new strategies and technologies to keep your business competitive and relevant.

Analytics and Data: Regularly analyze your data and performance metrics to identify areas for improvement and optimization.

Testing and Experimentation: Continue to A/B test different strategies, content formats, and promotions to refine your approach.

Scaling your affiliate marketing business requires a combination of strategic planning, delegation, diversification, and a commitment to ongoing learning and adaptation. By implementing these strategies, you can expand your reach, increase your earnings, and build a sustainable affiliate marketing business.

Chapter 10: Affiliate Marketing Success Stories

Success stories in affiliate marketing can offer valuable insights and inspiration to aspiring affiliate marketers. In this chapter, we will explore inspiring case studies, lessons learned from successful affiliate marketers, and real-life affiliate marketing journeys.

Inspiring Case Studies

Examining successful affiliate marketing case studies can provide you with practical examples of what works. Some key areas to explore in case studies include:

Niche Selection: Learn how successful affiliates chose profitable niches and identified audience needs.

Content Strategies: Understand their content creation strategies, including the types of content they produce and their content promotion methods.

Promotion Techniques: Explore their affiliate promotion techniques, such as SEO, social media, email marketing, and paid advertising.

Conversion Strategies: Discover how they optimize their websites and content to maximize conversions.

Scaling Efforts: Learn how these affiliates scaled their businesses over time, from their initial efforts to their current successes.

Lessons from Successful Affiliate Marketers

Successful affiliate marketers have valuable insights to share. Here are some common lessons from their experiences:

Patience and Persistence: Success often takes time. Be patient and keep refining your strategies.

Continuous Learning: Stay updated with industry trends and technologies to adapt to changes.

Content Quality: Focus on providing high-quality, valuable content that genuinely helps your audience.

Relationship Building: Build strong relationships with affiliate program managers and other affiliates in your niche.

Diversification: Diversify your income streams to mitigate risks associated with relying on one program or niche.

Testing and Optimization: Regularly test and optimize your strategies for better results.

Real-Life Affiliate Marketing Journeys

Real-life affiliate marketing journeys offer a glimpse into the ups and downs of affiliate marketing careers. These stories often include:

Initial Challenges: Discover the challenges and setbacks they faced when starting their affiliate marketing journeys.

Turning Points: Learn about pivotal moments or strategies that led to their breakthroughs and success.

Mistakes Made: Understand the mistakes they made along the way and the lessons learned from them.

Achievements: Celebrate their achievements and milestones as they progressed in their affiliate marketing careers.

Advice for Beginners: Gain valuable advice and tips they offer to newcomers in the field.

By studying success stories, learning from experienced affiliate marketers, and following the journeys of real-life affiliates, you can gain inspiration, insights, and guidance to chart your own path to success in affiliate marketing. Remember that every journey is unique, and there's no one-size-fits-all approach, but learning from others' experiences can be immensely valuable.

Conclusion

In the concluding chapter of this guide, we'll recap the key takeaways you've learned throughout your affiliate marketing journey, discuss the importance of embracing this exciting career path, and offer final words of encouragement to empower you on your affiliate marketing adventure.

Recap of Key Takeaways

Throughout this guide, you've delved into the world of affiliate marketing and gained a wealth of knowledge, including:

Understanding Affiliate Marketing: You've learned what affiliate marketing is and how it works, from joining affiliate programs to earning commissions.

Creating Valuable Content: You've explored the importance of creating high-quality, engaging content that resonates with your target audience.

Market Research and Targeting: You've discovered the significance of market research, audience targeting, and the validation of your creative ideas.

Crafting a Unique Value Proposition: You've mastered the art of crafting a compelling value proposition and brand story.

Building a Strong Brand: You've understood the essentials of branding and the importance of consistency.

Business Planning and Strategy: You've developed a creative business plan, set realistic goals, and grasped financial planning for creatives.

Legalities and Business Structure: You've navigated legal considerations, intellectual property, and licensing matters.

Funding Your Creative Venture: You've explored funding options, from bootstrapping to external funding.

Marketing and Promotion: You've embraced digital marketing, content strategies, and community-building.

Sales and Pricing Strategies: You've learned to set the right prices, employ effective sales techniques, and handle rejection and negotiation.

Customer Relationship Management: You've focused on building strong client relationships and handling feedback.

Scaling and Growth: You've explored strategies for expanding your creative business and managing growth challenges.

Overcoming Creative Blocks and Burnout: You've discovered how to navigate the creative process, deal with burnout, and stay inspired.

Sustainability and Social Responsibility: You've explored ethical business practices and sustainability in the creative industry.

Navigating Challenges and Adversities: You've learned about common challenges and the importance of resilience and adaptation.

Success Stories: You've been inspired by the journeys and lessons of successful creative entrepreneurs.

The Future of Creative Entrepreneurship: You've glimpsed into the future, considering trends, opportunities, and the ever-evolving landscape.

Embracing Your Affiliate Marketing Journey

Affiliate marketing is an ever-evolving field filled with opportunities for creativity, growth, and financial success. As you embark on your journey, remember that:

Passion and Persistence Matter: Your dedication to your niche and your willingness to persist through challenges are keys to your success.

Adaptability is Key: The affiliate marketing landscape is dynamic. Be open to adapting your strategies and learning from your experiences.

Value and Ethics Count: Providing real value to your audience and adhering to ethical practices are fundamental to long-term success.

Final Words of Encouragement

Your affiliate marketing journey is a path of learning, growth, and limitless potential. You have the knowledge, strategies, and insights needed to succeed. As you navigate this exciting career, keep your passion alive, embrace new opportunities, and remember that every step forward brings you closer to your goals. Affiliate marketing is a journey worth embarking on, and with determination and dedication, you can achieve the success you envision. Best of luck on your affiliate marketing adventure!

Acknowledgments

A creative endeavor, such as writing a book on creative entrepreneurship, is not a solitary pursuit. It involves the contributions, support, and inspiration of many individuals and resources. We would like to express our heartfelt gratitude to those who have played a significant role in bringing this book to fruition.

Our Thanks Go To:
God Almighty

Creative Minds: To all the creative entrepreneurs and artists who generously shared their experiences, insights, and stories. Your contributions have enriched the content of this book and inspired countless others on their entrepreneurial journeys.

Mentors and Advisors: To the mentors and advisors who provided guidance, expertise, and valuable feedback throughout the writing process. Your wisdom and experience have been invaluable.

Readers and Supporters: To the readers and supporters who have shown interest in this book from its inception. Your enthusiasm and encouragement have been a driving force in our commitment to creating a valuable resource.

Family and Friends: To our families and friends for their unwavering support, patience, and understanding during the long hours spent crafting this book. Your belief in us has been a constant source of motivation.

Publishing Team: To the publishing team, editors, and professionals who helped shape and refine this manuscript. Your expertise and dedication have transformed ideas into a coherent narrative.

The Creative Community: To the entire creative community, both established and emerging, for your boundless creativity and passion. You inspire us every day.

Remember that creativity is a collaborative endeavor, and your contributions to the world of art and entrepreneurship are invaluable. We hope this book serves as a source of knowledge, inspiration, and empowerment for all creative entrepreneurs on their remarkable journeys.

With heartfelt gratitude,

[Simeon Favour]